KEEPING *the* TRUTH ALIVE

Cory P. McLiechey

© 2021 Cory P. McLiechey. All rights reserved.

No part of this book may be reproduced, stored in a retrieval system, or transmitted by any means without the written permission of the author.

AuthorHouse™
1663 Liberty Drive
Bloomington, IN 47403
www.authorhouse.com
Phone: 833-262-8899

Because of the dynamic nature of the Internet, any web addresses or links contained in this book may have changed since publication and may no longer be valid. The views expressed in this work are solely those of the author and do not necessarily reflect the views of the publisher, and the publisher hereby disclaims any responsibility for them.

This book is printed on acid-free paper.

ISBN: 978-1-6655-3242-6 (sc)
ISBN: 978-1-6655-3243-3 (e)
ISBN: 978-1-6655-3749-0 (hc)

Library of Congress Control Number: 2021914664

Print information available on the last page.

Published by AuthorHouse 09/08/2021

authorHOUSE®

Reference Page

Neil Irvin Painter-(A life a symbol published 1996)

Thomas Mcliechey (family historian/artist)

Shawn Jones Durr (my cousin) and family historian of the Jones/Durr family structure.

Derrick Hatten

research/development/marketing asst.

Javonte Tubbs – interior proof read/grammatical edits

Gina Mcliechey-(my sister) research/development asst.

To my Great Niece
To: Harmony!

Always remember you come from greatness. The truth is powerful and it prevails! You are the future Nwery

Sincerely yours,
Love uncle
Cong. M[...]

Keeping the Truth Alive!
Introduction

This is a nursery rhyme style children's book about an iconic historical figure in American History. Her name is Sojourner Truth! Although the book is written in a style suitable for ages 3-12, the information in this American History educational book, which is very seldom told, can be useful for all ages. This is a nursery rhyme style timeline of the trials and tribulations of an enslaved Heroine who stood tall against her oppressor, and fought against inequality, racism, and injustice. She fought the system that re-captured her son and subjugated him back into the institution of slavery. She also beat a murder trial, which was next to impossible for a 'Black' person during her time. This children's book is only a fraction of the many things that Sojourner Truth has accomplished and endured. This book is dedicated to my parents:

Benjamin F. Mcliechey

(Born 2-13-1932 / Died 1-29-2021)

Ruth M. Mcliechey

(Born 7-22-1936 / Died 5-8-2021)

and also a special adopted mother of mine whom I never had the pleasure of meeting, her name was *SHAHEENA ISMAIL KHAN* She is the mother of Moshin Khan who digitally enhanced my illustrations. She died just 3 days after my mother died. May God accept them all in the hereafter Ameen!

R.I.P. Love your son Cory Mcliechey!

Acknowledgements

I would first like to start by thanking my cousin **Shawn Jones Durr**. She helped me learn about my Grandmother Irene Jones, who soon became **Irene McLiechey** after marrying **Thomas Mcliechey** in the late 1800s. **Shawn** and I both were equally amazed by our family lineage and the blood-lines that we are attached to. Shawn's father **Bobby Jones** married Malcolm X's youngest sister **Yvonne Little**. She later gave birth to three children who are my second and third generation blood cousins. **Shawn** and her siblings are blood related nephews and nieces of the late great **Malcolm X (El Hajj Maliq Shabazz)**. This also makes **Sojourner Truth** their Great Great Great Aunt through marriage. Shawn searched through Ancestry.com using her sister's login and discovered information about **Sojourner Truth** in her family tree. My Grandma **Irene** and her Grandpa (my uncle) **Benny** are brother and sister. **Frank Mcliechey** married **Fannie Schuyler** and they gave birth to **Thomas Mcliechey** and he met my grandmother **Irene Jones** and the rest is history!

Shout out to my brother/sister **Ben** and **Trinh Troung Mcliechey**. The both of you held me down years before all this came into a thought. Whenever I needed a little extra padding you two always came through in the clutch. I appreciate the both of you very much! ♥

To my kids **C'aira, Cory, London** and **Khyree** always remember you come from greatness and never let anything stop you from achieving your goals ! ♥♥♥♥ To my nieces and nephews ♥ **Sheena, Cc, Taneka, Tyreeka, Tania, Ericka, Amoni, Derrica, Mike T, Dee dee, Tawana, Reek, Jacoi, Darrick, Torrey, Bian, Norman, Tiaz,** 60+ this is also for you. Learn who you come from to understand where you can go in life. There is no limit to what you can achieve!

I am a Descendent of the Truth, Sojourner was her name!

Born Isabella Baumfree to Mama Bett and Father James.

The year was 1797, but the birthdate isn't known to be exact.

Birth records weren't recorded in these times, just one of the many true facts.

In 1806, at the tender age of nine, Isabella was sold with a flock of sheep during this time.

In 1808, Isabella was bought by Matinus Schryver. Her father made a visit to see her. In him she confided. With hopes to make a bad situation better, He kept his promise and had someone come and get her.

In 1815, Isabella fell in love with an enslaved man named Robert. Unexpectedly and against Robert's kidnappers rules, they shared the birth of a daughter. They named her Diana. They would never see one another again as Robert's kidnappers beating brought Robert's life to an end.

In 1817, she was forced to marry an enslaved man named Thomas. It wasn't based on love but to him she was honest. As time went on she gave birth to five children; Peter, Diana, Elizabeth and Sophia were named after her siblings. I know this is only four when I said it was five, but her first child, James, was a still born and didn't survive.

In 1826, Isabella walked away to her freedom carrying her youngest daughter.

Her kidnapper reneged on an agreement he made to release her from his clutches with honor.

His excuse was her severed finger from a year prior prevented her from producing the numbers he desired.

Her actions spoke louder than her words and that was crucial.

That's why she walked away from that place realizing it was her God-given right to do so!

In 1828, Isabella won back her son Peter after going through several Federal court proceedings. He was kidnapped and sold back into slavery in the Southern region. The Grand Jury returned her son to her. Isabella was delighted to see him.

In 1829, Isabella moved to New York with her son Peter. It was just a feeling she had, no one showed up there to greet her. She was a strong woman inside and out. This was the city to make a better life for her and Peter, no doubt!

In 1835, a religious leader implied that Isabella murdered someone. She was put on trial and with substantial evidence her case was won. She also counter sued her accuser for slander. The judge granted her appeal, it seems that her prayers were answered.

Between 1840-1841, Isabella received five letters from her son Peter. He worked on a whaler ship, and it wasn't often that he would see her.

When the ship return to dock in 1842, Peter was nowhere onboard and Isabella had no clue. What could have happened or where could he be?

Not realizing the last time she saw her son was the last time before he sailed out to sea.

In 1843, at the age of 46 Isabella changed her name to Sojourner Truth, and it was a perfect fit.

In 1844, Sojourner Truth joined the North-Hampton Association of Abolitionists. Floyd Garrison, Jolene Gilbert, Frederick Douglass which were a few names on this short list.

In 1850, Sojourner Truth dictated her book to Olive Gilbert. The Narratives of a Northern Slave. This was a means of supporting herself among the other financial paths that she paved.

In 1851, Sojourner Truth joined a Speakers Bureau run by a man named George Thompson. May 29th, this same year, she gave her famous speech "Ain't I A Woman."

In 1856, Sojourner Truth moved to Battle Creek. She bought her first home, and continues to travel the land to speak.

In 1864, after the Civil War ended, she worked with the Freedman's Bureau to help black men and women, find resources to create a better means of living.

She spoke to then President, Abraham Lincoln, which "seemed" pretty cool.

She requested land out West for minorities... 40 acres and a mule!

In 1883, Sojourner died after coming down ill with infected wounds on her legs. People that once met her couldn't believe she was dead. Though her physical frame is gone her spirit and energy live on. Through her bloodline descendants like Myself her fifth generation Grandson!

Cory P. McLiechey

Carrying the Torch

Honorable mention and congrats goes out to these exceptional women and over achievers in their respective fields as we honorably recognize them as Descendants of the Truth which is a Movement in itself -

Esmeralda Simmons

- Occupation: Executive Director of the Center for Law and Social Justice at Medgar Evers College
- Location: Brooklyn, NY
- Cause: Quality Public Education for students of color

Esmeralda Simmons has been engaged in the fight for equal rights for more than three decades. As a civil rights lawyer, she has worked in the U.S. Department of Education, for a federal judge, and throughout New York state and City Governments. Simmons now runs the Center for Law and Social Justice at Medgar Evers College in Brooklyn, which provides legal services to people facing voter suppression and discrimination.

Michelle Alexander

- Occupation: Law Professor at Ohio State University
- Location: Columbus, OH
- Cause: Fighting racial oppression

Michelle Alexander's book, "The New Jim Crow: Mass Incarceration in the Age of Colorblindness" argued that the racial oppression of the 20th century had been replaced by a new system of racial oppression – prisons, filled disproportionately with black men. The book has become a must-read for civil rights activists, according to a foreword of the book by Harvard University Public Philosophy Professor Dr. Cornel West. Alexander, who is a civil rights lawyer, has litigated numerous class action discrimination cases.

Lateefah Simon

- Occupation: President of the Akonadi Foundation
- Location: San Francisco Bay Area, Calif.
- Cause: Racial justice

In 2003, when she was just 26, Lateefah Simon won a MacArthur genius grant for her work helping impoverished and formerly incarcerated women. She has kept fighting against injustice and working in marginalized communities, helping young activists thrive. Today, Simon runs the Akonadi Foundation, which works to eliminate structural inequalities and create a just society.

Melanie Campbell

- Occupation: CEO of the National Coalition on Black Civic Participation
- Location: Washington, D.C.
- Cause: Civic Engagement

Melanie Campbell has worked for youth rights and women's rights for more than two decades. She was recognized as one of Washington D.C.'s Top 40 Under 40 Emerging Leaders in 2000. Campbell has helped create a youth-focused leadership development program called Black Youth Vote! This played a key role in the 2012 election, when the 66.2% of eligible black voters who participated in the election surpassed white, hispanic and Asian voting rates for the first time in history.

Dr. Charity Clay

Dr. Charity Clay is a Critical Race Sociologist of the African Diaspora. She received her PhD. in Sociology from Texas A&M University in 2014. She is currently an assistant professor at Xavier University of Louisiana, an HBCU in New Orleans where she heads the concentration in crime and Social Justice.

As an educator, she uses sociological perspectives to help her students understand systems of oppression and resistance at micro and macro levels. She is passionate about developing students' skills to conduct, analyze and apply qualitative and quantitative research as tools of resistance.

As a researcher her interests center around pressing issues throughout the African Diaspora including but not limited to, impacts of constructing Black Womanhood through the white gaze, the importance of African Descended students having global education experiences, Gentrification as Structural Racial Oppression, The significance of the Caribbean in strengthening cultural connections from Africa to the United States, and the impacts of Social Media on Black Resistance. Dr.Clay also serves on the Advisory Board of Descendants of the Truth as well as holding the role of director for the D.O.T. in the Southwest region of the U.S.

CONGRATULATIONS- Zaila Avante Garde, she is a basketball prodigy and holds 3 Guinness book world records at the age of 14 years old. She made history July 8th, 2021 becoming the 1st African American in 96 years to win the Scripps National Spelling Bee.

Thank you's

Thank you to **Dr. Betty Shabazz** and Brother **Malcolm X (El Hajj Maliq Shabazz) Ilyasah Shabazz** and siblings. I personally appreciate the many sacrifices made by this royal African American family as well as all the many examples of humility, kindness and perseverance representing what it truly means to be united in America no matter your race, gender or creed. No matter what obstacles and roadblocks are placed before you, we still can coexist, succeed, and learn to love one another.

Thank you **Vinnie Bagwell** for your words of wisdom and encouragement to challenge myself and achieve the hard goals giving persistent attention to the task before me; paying attention to the details in life, as you say, because that's where the Truth lies.

Thank you to my cousin **Burl C. Mcliechey** who always encouraged me over the years to carry the torch for the family as a representative and speaker on behalf of the Sojourner Truth Movement; and to always try and keep her legacy remembered and relevant.

Thank You to my cousin **Thomas 'Wish' Mcliechey,** sometimes I call him **'Wishbone'**. He's 82 years old and he is the family historian. I was first introduced to Sojourner Truth when I was about 5yrs old. 'Wish' would post these plaques on the trees at our family reunions. I was curious about what he was doing, but too young to understand that I came from greatness! 'Wish' has great passion for his ancestors and I thank him for preserving our legacy. Love you cuz!

Thank You to my big bro **Lateef " Cal " Calloway** for taking on the task of reintroducing my great ancestor/ Grandmother (5) Sojourner Truth to the world with a documentary/movie/tv series in the making. Thanks for the motivation and influence you had on me to reignite my art skills and put them to use. You know we accept you as her honorary Grandson...CMB 4 life ♥♥♥♥!

To my crew **Charles Trotter** and **Jessie Crawford (Top Notch Painting LLC)** I personally appreciate both of your support for helping me remain profitable and to be able to make meetings out of state. While you handle the operations of the business. Allowing me to function efficiently in other areas of my life that are demanding.. FOE ♥♥♥♥

A special thanks to my brother **Moshin Khan** who formatted my book and digitized my illustrations. We started on this journey together in February of 2021 meeting through a social business app online. We had no idea how significant our brotherhood would become when our mothers died just 3 days apart; yours in Pakistan and mines in the U.S. It made this project that much more meaningful and important to us and how we honor these phenomenal women who gave us birth. May God be pleased with your time here on earth Umi Ameen ♥!

Thank you elder Taalib El Amin for the stories you shared of my father from your perspective as a youth and the advice and guidance you give to me and our community as a whole. You are the example for the generation behind you to set the example for those that will come after my generation. You are a priceless gem to the world ♥ community♥ !

Thank you **Mayor Bill de Blasio** for your involvement and influence with the Artist Corps which directly impacts artist like Vinnie Bagwell as well as benefits performances, public artworks, pop up shows throughout New York ie- It's Time FOR HIP HOP IN NYC 2021. Which was a great success!

Extra special Thank You to **Rocky Bucano** for taking on the larger than life task of preserving Hip Hop on a **Universal** scale. I was born in 1973 in GrandRapids, MI and I am **Hip Hop** as I stated to you upon initially being introduced to you by **Jennifer Mczier** ♥(our mutual friend whom I share an invaluable friendship with **#theoracle**). This nursery rhyme style children's book is a nod to all the great legends who were single handedly instrumental in the birth of **Hip Hop: "Melle Mel" Grandmaster Flash & the Furious Five, Dj Kool Herc, Kool Dj Rock** and **Kurtis Blow** just to name a few. The phonetic melody of this Book encouraged by the rhyming phrases was first introduced to me by these legends. Respect to the female legends as well that followed such as **Roxanne Shante, Mc Lyte, Queen Latifah,** and **Lauryn Hill** just to name a few. So I was inspired to incorporate Hip Hop into this body of work assisting me with telling the story of this incredible woman. This was intentional as we believe this method could help the children to remember the facts of this iconic woman as well as having fun learning about her. May it also encourage a deep understanding of self.

www.descendantsofthetruth.com